OUR WILDLIFE WORLD

ELEPHANTS

Elin Kelsey

Grolier

FACTS IN BRIEF

Classification of the elephant
    Class: *Mammalia* (mammals)
    Order: *Proboscidea* (animals with proboscises)
    Family: *Elephantidae* (elephant family)
    Genus: *Loxodonta* and *Elephas*
    Species: *Loxodonta africana* (African Elephant); *Elephas maximus* (Asian or Indian Elephant)

World distribution.   Asia and Africa.

Habitat.   Forest, plains and marshes.

Distinctive physical characteristics.   Loose-fitting gray skin, long prehensile trunk; both male and female African elephants have tusks, usually only male Asian elephants have them.

Habits.   Females and young live together in small herds, males live alone or in small all-male groups. Elephants forage constantly in order to get enough to eat and so must keep moving around.

This series is approved and recommended by the Federation of Ontario Naturalists.

Canadian Cataloguing in Publication Data

Kelsey, Elin
  Elephants

(Nature's children)
Issued also in French under title: L'éléphant.
Includes index.
ISBN 0-7172-2484-8

1. Elephants—Juvenile literature.   I. Title.   II. Series.

QL737.P98K44 1988   j599.6'1   C88-094676-8

Contents

The last time you went to a movie they were probably selling jumbo-sized drinks, bags of popcorn and candy bars. Did you ever stop to wonder how the word ''jumbo'' came to mean extra large?

Jumbo was the name of a very famous elephant. He was one of the first elephants to appear in an American circus. Everyone who met Jumbo was fascinated by his incredible size and fell in love with his gentle and charming personality. To know Jumbo was to love him. Although Jumbo was in many ways unique, elephants *are* very special animals. Read on to find out why.

The elephant is our largest land animal.

Elephant I.D.

Although some elephants come from Africa and others from Asia, you can recognize any elephant by its huge body and wrinkled trunk.

The easiest way to tell where an elephant comes from is to look at its ears. An African elephant's ears are truly enormous. In fact, they are nearly twice as large as the ears of an Asian elephant.

The shape of an elephant's body also provides important clues. Asian elephants' high, round heads and arched backs give them a chubby appearance. African elephants have low, rather flat foreheads and their backs are slightly U-shaped. Also, the head of an African elephant hangs below its shoulders, while the Asian elephant holds its head higher.

Can you tell what kind of elephants these are?

6

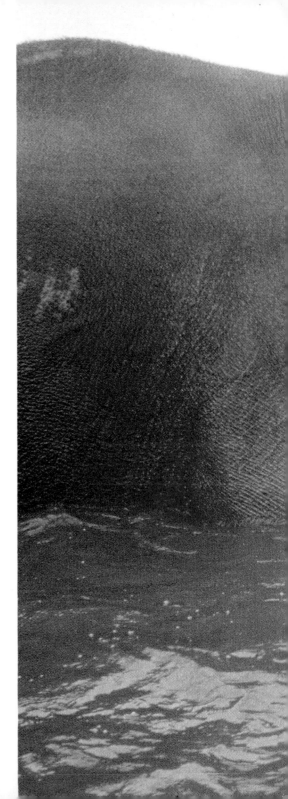

Elephant-Land

Elephants live in tropical countries where it is warm all year round. For most of the year the weather is hot and dry. But during the rainy season it is very wet.

Most African elephants live south of the Sahara Desert in open grassy areas called savannas. However, with the exception of the desert areas, elephants have been found in every kind of African environment, including rocky mountain slopes. Asian elephants are found in India, Sri Lanka, South China and Southeast Asia. They live mainly in forested areas.

Opposite page: The elephant's pillar-like legs are designed to support its great weight.

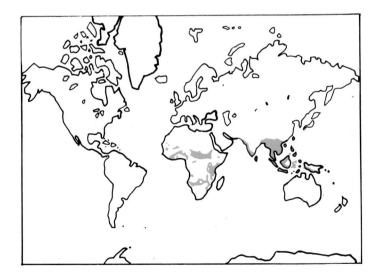

The shaded area on this map shows where elephants live.

African elephant.

Asian elephant.

Jumbo Sized

If elephants played basketball they would have a distinct advantage. A full-grown male African elephant is so tall he could look *down* into the basketball net! An Asian male elephant would have to be careful, though. He's just the right height to bump his head on the hoop.

Not only are elephants tall, they are also very heavy. A male African elephant can weigh up to 6000 kilograms (13 000 pounds), which is about five or six times as much as your family car! The lighter Asian male averages about 4500 (10 000 pounds).

Female elephants are usually smaller than the males and weigh quite a bit less.

The only hair on an elephant's body is at the tip of its tail, which serves as a handy fly swatter.

Gigantic Appetites

An elephant's enormous size is matched by its gigantic appetite. If you were to invite an elephant over for salad, it could eat more than 900 platefuls! And it needs almost a bathtub full of water a day to wash it all down!

An elephant needs so much food that it usually spends at least 16 hours a day eating. This means that by the time it reaches its sixtieth birthday, an elephant may have spent 40 years of its life eating!

Elephants will eat a wide variety of plants and fruit but they do have particular favorites. African elephants love grass—up to 90 percent of their diet is grass. They also snack on tree bark and fruit. Asian elephants feed mainly on leaves, plant roots, flowers and bamboo.

An elephant uses its tusks to strip tasty bark off a tree.

Teeth

If you've ever munched on a stringy piece of celery, you'll have some idea of what elephant food is like. It needs a lot of chewing before it can be swallowed. Elephants are well equipped to chew up all this tough food. Here's how.

Throughout your life, you will have two sets of teeth—your baby and then your adult teeth. Elephants, on the other hand, have six sets of teeth!

Only four of an elephant's gigantic brick-shaped teeth, called molars, are in use at any one time. These molars can be found one on each side of the upper and lower jaw. They first come in at the back of the jaw and slowly move forward as they are needed. In other words, when the tooth in the front is worn down and falls out, there's another one ready to take its place.

Because it has such a short neck, the elephant can't reach the ground with its mouth, so it must rely on its trunk to pick up food.

Trusty Tusks

An elephant's tusks are actually huge, pointed, ivory teeth that keep on growing throughout the elephant's life. Both male and female African elephants have long white tusks. In some large males, each tusk may weigh as much as your mom or dad. Male Asian elephants have smaller tusks, and often the females do not have tusks at all.

Elephants put their tusks to many different uses. They use them to dig for roots and to peel the bark off trees. When water is scarce they drill for water in dry river beds with their tusks. Occasionally they will even use them as weapons. And when things are peaceful, tusks make a great trunk rest.

Overleaf:
When an elephant and rhino meet they usually go about their own business.

Only two-thirds of an elephant's tusk is visible, the rest is embedded in the skull.

Wondrous Trunks

Have you ever played "push the penny" with your nose? It isn't easy. Your nose is so small that it is difficult to make it do much more than breathe, smell and occasionally wiggle. But an elephant's nose is something else again!

An elephant's nose together with its upper lip form a flexible trunk that can be used for just about everything. Imagine being able to scratch, lift, carry, throw, touch, smell, shower and hug —all using your nose!

The end of the trunk is as sensitive as your fingertips. With it, an elephant can pick up a single blade of grass. An elephant's trunk contains more than 40 000 muscles and tendons, which make it very strong and flexible. That's why elephants can also use their trunks to lift heavy logs or to push down tasty-looking trees.

One of the most important uses for a trunk, however, is to smell. By sticking its trunk in the air an elephant can keep aware of danger. It can also smell ripe fruit as far as four city blocks away! Yum.

Opposite page:
The tip of the Asian elephant's trunk has one small fleshy "finger," unlike that of the African elephant which has two.

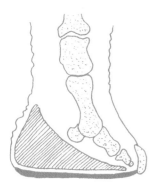

X-ray of an elephant's foot.

Elephants on the Move

An elephant needs so much food and water that it may have to travel great distances to find enough. Most of the time an elephant strolls along at about the same speed as you jog. Should something startle it, however, it can race away at 40 kilometres (25 miles) an hour.

Would you believe that an elephant can move around almost silently when it wants to? It's true. Although elephants have enormous feet —some are bigger than serving platters—they are not loud and clumsy. In fact, the special design of their feet allows them to walk quietly and gracefully.

If you saw an X-ray of an elephant's foot, you would notice that the toe bones are permanently pointed on tiptoe. A fatty, elastic pad beneath the toes and heel forms a spongy cushion that enables the elephant to walk almost silently, leaving hardly any tracks. Ridges on the sole of an elephant's foot help it to get a good grip on rocky slopes or when climbing out of slippery mud holes.

Opposite page:
An elephant convoy.

22

Elephant Roads

Elephants travel on special trails. Many of these were first made hundreds of years earlier by the elephant's great-great-great-grandparents. Each trail leads to a favorite feeding area or watering hole.

Traveling elephants move in an orderly single file. As if marching in a parade, each one carefully places its feet one in front of the other. Elephants step so carefully that their trails remain very narrow—just wide enough for them to squeeze through.

Elephant mothers make sure their youngsters stay very near them on the trail. A baby elephant will walk between its mother's front legs. When it gets a little older it will hang on to her tail, now and then receiving a helpful pull if the path becomes steep or slippery.

Keeping Cool

If you want to find an elephant at noon on a sweltering hot day, start by looking under a tall tree. Whenever it can, that's where an elephant will go spend the midday hours resting in the shade to avoid overheating. And if it gets really hot, an elephant has a very special way of cooling down: it waves its ears!

An elephant's ears are full of blood vessels. By flapping its ears, an elephant cools down the blood that circulates through them. The cooled blood is then pumped back through the elephant, lowering the temperature of its entire body.

African elephants have larger ears than the forest-dwelling Asian elephants. That is because African elephants live in open grassy areas where they can't always find shade. They need larger ears to help them keep cool. Each of an African elephant's enormous ears weighs about twice as much as you do!

"I'm all ears!"

Mud Baths

Most of us like to take bubble baths. Elephants like to bathe too, but instead of bubble baths they take mud baths! Skidding, rolling and splashing, a group of elephants will wallow in a gooey mud hole until they are covered from trunk to toe.

It looks like great fun and it probably is, but it serves a useful purpose too. The skin of an elephant looks tough and leathery, but it is actually very sensitive. A nice thick coat of mud goes a long way towards protecting it from the hot, drying sun and irritating insect bites. And just in case that is not sufficient, an elephant will often follow its bath with a powdering of dust for extra bug protection!

An elephant takes a dust bath by sucking dirt up its trunk and blowing it out over itself.

Everybody in the Pool

Elephants head for water whenever they get the chance. They enjoy playing in water and they also drink enormous quantities of it. They do not suck it up through their trunks as some people think. They use their trunks to hold the water before squirting it into their mouths. They also shower their backs with water to cool themselves.

Believe it or not, these gigantic animals are excellent swimmers! They often swim underwater with only their trunks and the tips of their ears above the surface. An elephant's trunk functions like a diver's snorkel. With its trunk held up, an elephant can swim underwater for hours and travel great distances.

"Come on in, the water's fine!"

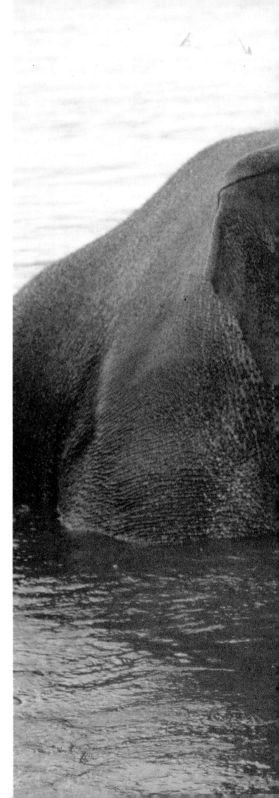

The Right Moves

Elephants have special ways of communicating. Just as your facial expression reflects your mood, the position of an elephant's head, ears, tail and trunk show how the elephant is feeling.

Friends often shake hands or hug when they meet each other. How do elephant friends say hello? They like to sniff each other and drape their trunks over one another's backs or wrap their trunks together.

A curious elephant will cock its ears forward and lift its trunk high in the air. If it smells something exciting it will flap its ears back and forth. If it senses danger it will spread its ears out and rap on the ground with its trunk as a warning.

Elephant Talk

As well as body language elephants use sounds to communicate. And since they are very sociable animals they make a lot of different sounds depending on what's happening.

The best-known elephant sound is trumpeting. This noise comes through the trunk to make it extra loud. It means that an elephant is excited, surprised, ready to attack or has become separated from the herd.

If an elephant is feeling contented, it will hang its trunk down straight and produce a rumbling sound deep in its throat. The happy elephant is purring! Since elephants purr more often in areas where there are lots of trees and they can't see one another, scientists think it is the elephants' way of keeping track of one another.

Usually elephants make sounds that can be heard quite clearly. Scientists have recently discovered, however, that sometimes the noises may be so low that only other elephants can hear them. This may help them to "talk" over long distances.

Opposite page:
Sounding the trumpet.

Living Together

Normally elephants live in small family groups called herds. A herd may contain as many as fifty elephants but smaller groups are more common. The surprising thing about an elephant herd is that only female elephants and their children belong to it. Adult male elephants or bulls live alone or in very small groups.

The oldest and wisest female elephant in the herd is the leader. Since elephants can live to be more than sixty years old, a leader may be very experienced. It is her job to protect the herd from danger. Because she knows where to find the best watering holes and feeding areas, she decides where the group will travel.

Members of an elephant herd are extremely close. If one elephant is injured or ill, the others will nurse it back to health. If an elephant has difficulty walking, two elephants will use their strong bodies to support the injured animal from either side.

Asian elephants spend the hottest times of the day in shady woods.

A Baby is Born

If you have ever had to wait for a new baby in your family you know that nine months can be an awfully long time. But imagine this: elephant mothers are pregnant for almost two years!

Elephants don't have doctors to deliver their babies but they do receive lots of help. As the time of birth draws closer, the mother becomes the center of attention. The other female elephants stay close by her side. When the exciting moment arrives, they are there to help and they won't leave until the new baby is up on its feet.

The members of the herd keep a careful watch to make sure that nothing harms the baby. Since it is too weak to travel during the first few days of its life, the herd won't set out on the trail until the newcomer can keep up.

It takes a baby elephant about 6 months to learn how to use its trunk properly.

Big Babies

Elephants have big babies. A new baby elephant is about as tall as a three-year-old child and weighs 100 kilograms (220 pounds) or more. It is called a calf.

The first thing the hairy calf does is wobble to its feet in search of milk. It has a big appetite and drinks about 10 litres (40 cups) of milk every day. (In case you wondered, a baby elephant, like all baby mammals, nurses with its mouth, not its trunk.)

Although the young elephant may start eating plants in its second year, it will continue to drink its mother's milk until it is three or four years old. It grows quickly and by the age of six it will probably weigh ten times as much as when it was born.

Lunchtime!

Staying Safe

Because they are so big and powerful, adult elephants have no natural enemies. Baby elephants, however, sometimes need protection from the lions of the African plains or Asia's tigers. At the first sign of danger, the adult members of a herd will form a tight circle with all of the younger elephants in the center. Then the adults will trumpet loudly and thrust their ears out to the side, like enormous pairs of wings. Sometimes these outstretched ears make the elephant appear so much bigger, the enemy may turn and run away. Should the intruder linger too long, the largest elephants will press their ears tightly against their heads and charge!

Elephant cows are very attentive mothers and won't let any intruders near their young.

Growing Up

Young elephants are very playful. By the time they are a year old, they love to wrestle and tumble in the mud, poking each other with their trunks and squealing with delight.

The youngsters learn by exploring and by imitating the other members of the herd. An elephant mother is very loving and offers lots of encouragement. However, she is firm about good behavior. Should a calf throw a tantrum, a quick trunk slap usually settles things down.

An elephant continues to grow all its life, though much more slowly in later years. It will, however, be considered grown *up* at ten or so. At about that age, the male elephants leave the herd and travel alone or in small groups. The females stay with their mothers, aunts and grandmothers and soon begin raising families of their own.

Words to Know

Bull   A male elephant.

Calf   A young elephant.

Cow   A female elephant.

Herd   A group of animals traveling and feeding together.

Molars   Large blunt teeth that are used to grind food.

Nurse   To drink milk from a mother's body.

Savanna   A grassy plain.

Snorkel   A breathing tube used by divers.

Tendon   A tough band of tissue that attaches a muscle to a bone or some other part.

Trunk   The long flexible snout of an elephant formed with the upper lip and the nose with the nostrils at the end.

Tusks   Special teeth that grow down out of the mouths of some animals such as elephants.

INDEX

Cover Photo: Art Gryfe, Network Stock Photo File

Photo Credits: Bob Wavra, page 4; Bill Ivy, pages 7, 21, 31; Chris Harvey, Masterfile, page 8; Robert Winslow, pages 11, 15, 25; William Smyth, page 12; Jack Templeton, page 16; Bradley Smith, Animals Animals, pages 18-19; Victor Burville, The Stock Market, page 23; B. Littlejohn, The Stock Market, page 26; John Rushmer, Hot Shots, pages 29, 33; Harvey Medland, Network Stock Photo, page 34; R. Homewood, page 37; Tony Stone Worldwide, Masterfile, page 39; Tony Stone Worldwide, The Stock Market, pages 40-41; Lori Labatt, Hot Shots, page 43; Boyd Norton, page 45.